PLEADERS AND PROTESTERS

THE FUTURE OF CITIZENS' ORGANIZATIONS IN ISRAEL

By Eliezer D. Jaffe

This monograph is one in a series of reports made possible by the Jacob Blaustein Institute for the Advancement of Human Rights of the American Jewish Committee in order to stimulate constructive discussion and interaction between Israelis and American Jews on concerns relevant to both societies.

*Copyright © 1980, The American Jewish Committee
Library of Congress Catalog No. 80-68431
ISBN No. 0-87495-028-7*

*Second Printing © 1982
Eliezer D. Jaffe
37 Gaza Road, Jerusalem 92 383*

All rights reserved. No part of this book may be reproduced in any form without written permission from the author except for brief passages in a review appearing in a newspaper or magazine.

Dedication

This book is dedicated to my sister and brother-in-law, Alice and Morris Zipkin, and to my brothers Alvin and Jack, as an expression of praise for their loyalty to the values and tradition of our parents, and for their involvement in Jewish communal work on behalf of our people and the State of Israel. May they and their children be privileged one day to live in Israel and participate personally in shaping the future of this country.

CONTENTS

Foreword   iv

Roles, Goals and Strategies   1

A Forecast for the Eighties   9

Zahavi: Anatomy of a Grass-roots Organization   16

Agenda for Leaders   27

Bibliography   35

FOREWORD

My purpose in writing this report on the development and the prospects of citizen involvement in Israel was not primarily academic. What I chiefly hoped to do was to inform both American Jews and Israelis about this important and rapidly changing section of the nation's life, and thereby encourage them to help in some way with the never-ending task of building a better Israel.

Thanks are due the Jacob Blaustein Institute for the Advancement of Human Rights, whose generosity made possible the publication of this report. The opinions expressed are, of course, strictly my own.

          E.D.J.

The Hebrew University
Jerusalem
September 1980

ROLES, GOALS AND STRATEGIES

Social change has many faces. It can be slow or sudden, gentle or violent; it can affect many people or just a few; it can be for the better or the worse. Israelis have always used party politics and the pursuit and power of public office in trying to change the conditions under which they lived; but during the last decade they have found three additional methods suitable for their society: social action, volunteerism and community organization. While the three differ in goals, strategies and the roles played by participants, all are increasingly attractive to Israelis and are increasingly employed by them.

Trends of the 1970s

During the last decade, citizen activity has burgeoned in Israel: as an expression of rising but unfulfilled expectations, of hopelessness and despair, and of the tradition of helping people in need. The appearance of the Israeli Black Panthers in 1971 and the misguided official reaction to them was one milestone; another was the mass demonstrations led by Motti Ashkenazi after the Yom Kippur War of 1973. Both events galvanized previously inert population groups into action and taught them the "power of the people."

The Black Panther episode began when a street-corner gang of young people from Musrara, a Jerusalem slum (since renamed Morasha, "heritage"), assembled in front of the City Hall to demand better housing, education and jobs as well as acceptance into the army,* despite having been denied a permit to demonstrate (Cromer, 1976). Earlier, municipal social workers had tried hard to get the Panthers off the street and into a clubhouse, but these kids were not out for personal gain. In their demonstration they took off with no holds barred, and confrontation with police escalated into violence. Prime Minister Golda Meir, alarmed, thereupon convened a committee of 129 experts who prepared the largely neglected <u>Prime Minister's Report on Disadvantaged Youth</u> (Prime Minister's Office, 1972), the first nationwide report on social conditions. This searching, comprehensive document, with its recommendations for remedial action, aroused widespread awareness of the problems and put grass-roots activism on the map as a political force.

---

*Youths with police records are usually rejected for service.

The Black Panther affair was also important in being an ethnic protest. Sephardi immigrants from Arab lands were demanding equal treatment and opportunity in a Western-dominated, Ashkenazi society. They were calling on ethnic brothers and sisters, in Israel and abroad, to join the struggle of the Sephardi disadvantaged. They were rejecting assimilation into the Ashkenazi culture and demanding a place of their own in the life of the country. The Panthers eventually committed political suicide by turning themselves into a rather impotent political party, which managed to gain exactly one seat in the Ninth Knesset, and that only by teaming up with the Communists; but they left a legacy of ethnic self-awareness among many Sephardi (and some Ashkenazi) Jews, and of respect for social action by underprivileged citizens.

Motti Ashkenazi, who led the demonstrations after the Yom Kippur War, was and is respected as a hero of that war. The military outpost he commanded, on the Bar Lev Line at the Suez Canal, was one of a very few to hold out against the Egyptian onslaught. Ashkenazi became totally convinced that Defense Minister Moshe Dayan's negligence was the cause of "Israel's Pearl Harbor" and demanded that Dayan resign from the Cabinet. However, a Committee of Inquiry, appointed by the Cabinet to investigate the events leading to the war, held that the Defense Minister was not specifically to blame, and he did not resign. At that point, Ashkenazi -- normally reticent and mild-mannered -- set up a vigil demanding "ministerial accountability" in front of the Prime Minister's office, and during the weeks that followed, he was joined by hundreds and then thousands in massive, peaceful protest demonstrations. In the end, Golda Meir herself stepped down, and with her the entire Cabinet.

The Black Panther affair and Ashkenazi's protest highlighted the power of citizens to influence social policies and the political system. They led to changes in government and to the emergence of political parties, such as that of Yigal Yadin. In the next election, all parties, including Mr. Begin's Likud, concentrated their appeals on internal issues and social problems. Unfortunately, the realities of governing by coalition have disappointed many Israelis, perhaps including politicians who had earlier talked earnestly and fervently about their plans to bridge social gaps, reform the electoral process and curtail bureaucracy. Aside from Project Renewal, a potentially significant attempt to rehabilitate 160 slum neighborhoods housing 45,000 families, little has been accomplished for the disadvantaged in recent years (Jaffe, 1978; 1980a). On the contrary, rampant inflation and unemployment, worsened by ill-starred attempts to curb them, have intensified social problems and drastically weakened the social services.

Against this background of events, more and more Israelis have been seeking to involve themselves in national or local affairs, in hopes of influencing their social environment. Some view social conditions as norms or legitimate constraints; their strategy consists of helping individuals adjust to, or live with, things as they are. Others consider certain existing conditions harmful and try to reform or change them.

Which of several types of social involvement an individual will choose depends, in the long run, on his or her moral views, attitudes toward norms and conformity, creeds or belief systems, and ability to tolerate gaps between rhetoric and reality (Rein, 1970). With this in mind, let us look at the three new approaches to social change in Israel, their methods and goals and the groups they cater to.

Social Action

In Israel, social activists usually come from population groups at the client's end of a social problem. They try to influence policy, legislation, the allocation of resources, and the official attitude toward themselves; they demand alterations in the services offered to them and are often immediate beneficiaries of the changes they seek. They generally feel oppressed by existing norms, and they want not palliatives, but system-wide institutional change.

Organized assaults on public opinion are the hallmark of most social-action groups; dedicated personal involvement, without professional middlemen, is their driving force. Methods range from passive non-participation, hunger strikes and sit-ins to violence and clashes with law enforcement or other government agencies. The news media are heavily used to influence public opinion; staging out-of-the-ordinary, media-attracting events is the daily bread of social-action groups. Most of them will employ disruptive tactics and purposely escalate protests into confrontations.

Some of the many groups that use these methods, in varying degrees, are the Israeli Black Panthers, the Peace Now movement, Gush Emunim, the Ohalim Neighborhood Associations, the feminist movement, the Association for Large Families (Zahavi), some of the immigrant landsmannschaften, the Israeli Association of Social Workers, the Housing Now Association, the Slum Neighborhood Residents Association and the Landlords Association. Some of them are almost messianic in their fervor, and when two of these come up against each other with opposed goals -- say Gush Emunim vs. Peace Now -- it's best to stand back, because the sparks might fly. Such conflicts occur rather frequently between religious groups that close roads to protect the sanctity of Shabbat and secular groups objecting to such religious coercion.

Whatever the consequences, social-action groups are in Israel to stay. They have mushroomed in the soil of ethnic, religious, feminist and other group interests and ideologies. Civil disobedience has grown more prevalent as coalition governments have shown themselves vulnerable to it. True, confrontations have been overdone; so many groups have staged them so frequently that government and political figures have at times grown numb and insensitive to the issues presented. Nevertheless, the consensus seems to be that social action, especially by disadvantaged groups, is an important vehicle for social involvement and change in Israel.

Community Organization

One role social workers have played in countries around the world during the past 50 years is that of professional community organizer. Such organizers are social workers, often university-trained, who specialize in planning and advocacy on behalf of disadvantaged groups, relay information about social problems to political bodies, thereby influencing policymakers (Korazin, 1978), and serve as advocates for their clients, intervening between them and governmental or other agencies when rights are obscured or denied (Cloward and Elman, 1970). In accordance with the model of community organization, as defined by the American social-work educator Irving Spergel, the Israeli organizer performs vigorously as a mediator or ombudsman on behalf of dispossessed groups vis-a-vis public or voluntary bureaucracies as well as political structures (Spergel, 1975). He or she directly champions the interests of estranged or deviant, relatively powerless and, usually, inarticulate population sectors, and persuades members of other professional or elite groups to represent these interests.

Most Israeli community organizers are paid civil-service professionals working on behalf of client groups. The advent of four social-work schools -- at the Hebrew, Bar-Ilan, Tel Aviv and Haifa Universities -- gave scores of young Israelis an opportunity for involvement in social change through the study and practice of community organization. Bar-Ilan University has specialized in this area of social-work education (Loewenberg, 1978; Neipris, 1978).

The use of community organizers in Israel was introduced during the 1950s by Amidar, a government corporation established by the Ministry of Housing to build, rent and maintain low-rent homes for new immigrants (Amidar, 1964; Hoffert, 1962). The organizers' basic role was to help residents take care of their apartments and guarantee the upkeep of housing projects through tenant committees and self-help activities. The organizer in effect had the Government for both his employer and his major client. The Ministry of Social Welfare and the various municipalities soon recognized the need to integrate community organization into the field of social work, and today such workers are found in "divisions of community work" at each of the nearly 200 local public-welfare departments. They often work with neighborhood and citizens' councils, street-corner youth, and clubs for the elderly or other groups. Inevitably, the clients' need for advocacy arises to challenge the community workers, so that they are constantly beset by conflicting loyalties: to their clients, their municipal employers and the mayor.

The community workers' dilemma is compounded by the extreme ambivalence, to put it mildly, of many mayors and elected officials toward "excessive" efforts at independent community organization. When citizen groups attack City Hall policies, disrupt services and pressure for changes in the allocation of resources, it can spell trouble for mayors and other officials. Community organizers who are too successful are often accused of putting "their" municipalities, including the mayor and his political party, in an unfavorable light, and sometimes their efforts give rise to new political opposition groups.

Officials, including many Knesset members, fear that pressure groups created by community organizers will get out of hand, and often warn that "no one knows what all this may lead to." Most experienced observers find that citizen involvement commands a great deal of lip service, but that official support dwindles perceptibly when the citizen groups take up lobbying, political action and independent advocacy. So do government funds for neighborhoods, because they are almost invariably granted to municipal welfare offices, not directly to citizens' organizations. Since no private funds, or virtually none, are available to these organizations, indigenous efforts have often been delayed, as has the development of a new kind of community organizer not employed by local government.

The most memorable episode in which community organizers paid the piper took place in Jerusalem when the Black Panthers first appeared on the scene as a street-corner gang. Several organizers assigned to the neighborhood were suspected by city officials of giving the Panthers too much political guidance, and when the Panthers turned to street demonstrations that made headlines the world over, the organizers were blamed. It seemed so important to neutralize and perhaps punish them that the Ministry of Social Welfare* agreed to "exile" them to the bailiwick of the rival Ministry of Education: In a deal between Social Welfare and the municipality, the local Community Organization Division was transferred from the city's Social Welfare Department to the Education Department, where the organizers would be tucked away from their former colleagues under the supervision of a no-nonsense deputy mayor.

Initially, this plan was approved for six months, after which it was to be reassessed. Today, eight years later, the community organizers are part of a new municipal Youth and Sports Department (formerly a division of the Education Department) -- the only community workers outside a municipal welfare department. They have been posted to community centers around the city and completely separated from advocacy and social-action functions. Thus "rendered harmless," many of them wander about Jerusalem dejected and inconsolable. However, their salaries have been funded all along by the Ministry of Labor and Social Affairs -- presumably in hopes that some day, somehow, they will be restored to that Ministry.

All these limitations and hazards notwithstanding, many students continue to be attracted to community-organization work as a way of participating in, and promoting, social change.

---

* Renamed the Ministry of Labor and Social Services in 1977.

Volunteering

Volunteerism in Israel has been admirably described by Harry M. Rosen and there is no need to duplicate his work here. Volunteers are a very different breed from social activists and community organizers. Rosen defines them as "people who, of their own free will and without financial compensation, assist others, either on a one-to-one basis or through the medium of an organization such as a service agency or a voluntary association" (Rosen, 1979, p. 7). In Israel, volunteering to assist others in the most altruistic sense is a long-standing practice, as it has been throughout the centuries of the Diaspora.

Until 1972, every organization "made Shabbat" for itself in recruiting volunteers; there was no central address. That year, the Israel Voluntary Services Agency was created, reflecting Prime Minister Golda Meir's belief that many more people would volunteer if volunteering were better coordinated and organized. Ever since, the agency has been generously funded by the Government. Between 1972 and 1978, the Ministries of Education and of Labor and Social Affairs initiated ambitious volunteer programs of their own.

Alan S. York, coordinator of Bar-Ilan University's program for "volunteer organizers," describes the changing concept of volunteering (York, 1978, p. 104):

> Volunteerism has always played a central place in the communal structure of the Jews in the Diaspora and was of no less importance in the pre-State Jewish community in Israel. However, the establishment of the State in 1948 led to a reaction against voluntary initiative and organization, for statehood, with its values of universalistic bureaucracy, was seen as being antipathetic towards voluntary amateurism....The 1970's have witnessed a gradual but significant swing of the pendulum: government, and, to a lesser extent, professional workers have realized that there are services they cannot provide at all or that volunteers can give better, and so the interest in volunteers and volunteerism has increased.

In other words, recruiting volunteers is viewed by many government officials as a means of obtaining needed nonprofessional manpower for ongoing national and municipal programs in such areas as social service, education, health care and defense. Volunteers are invariably placed and supervised by professional workers or paid employees, who decide where they are needed and what they are to do.

Volunteering is of tremendous importance in the social service network, lessening the burdens of overworked staff and saving professional manpower at relatively low cost. To officialdom it is a much more acceptable form of citizen involvement than social activism or community organization, because it does not rely on confrontation, is guided by professional anchor people and helps government agencies do their jobs better. It is respectable and sought after, thanks to the high prestige of the host organizations, whether they are hospitals, government agencies, women's groups or organizations for the handicapped or underprivileged.

For all these reasons, this kind of relatively sustained effort to help fellow human beings attracts larger numbers of Israelis than do other forms of altruistic action: more than social-action groups, which function at the fringe of citizen effort and have to scrounge for funds, for recognition and often for survival; more than community organization, whose practitioners must shuttle nimbly between volunteers and social-action groups, serve as broker between clients and volunteers, and advise and support social-action groups in their demands -- all the time risking over-identification with social-action groups and the penalties therefor.

Individual, altruistic volunteerism in Israel stems not so much from a desire to change Israeli society structurally or politically as from a wish to make life easier for people in difficult situations. Many volunteers derive personal gratification from the one-to-one relationships with those they help; many find their reward in learning concretely about previously abstract problems through encounters with troubled individuals and families. There may well be more face-to-face volunteering in Israel than among Jewish communities in the U.S. and elsewhere in the Diaspora, where fund-raising often becomes the major mode and goal of Jewish philanthropy, where the eventual use of the funds raised is only dimly perceived and where there are few opportunities for personal involvement and for discerning use of oneself and one's money.

A FORECAST FOR THE EIGHTIES

Prophecy ended with the destruction of the Second Temple, we are taught; but forecasting is still in vogue. Social developments during the 1980s give us some indication of the directions citizen involvement in Israel may take in the 1980s. Four major trends stand out: Client groups have been getting more involved in the struggle for resources; social action has become more political and has increasingly relied on confrontation techniques; antagonism between grass-roots groups and government is on the increase; and volunteering in the accustomed forms has encountered some hard sledding.

The Growing Role of Client Groups

In the new decade, client groups and grass-roots movements will probably become more active at the neighborhood and the national level. Groups which until now let social workers speak for them will begin to speak out on their own behalf. This has already happened with organizations of large families, street-corner gangs, associations of parents of retarded persons and several other groupings. The aged will probably organize and begin to lobby, as will, for example, widows, the blind and families of psychiatric patients. Social workers and politicians, traditionally the "protectors" and mouthpieces of such groups, have proved too vulnerable to political pressures. They are at least one step removed from their clients' problems, and government officials and policymakers take them less seriously than they used to.

Three developments make it likely that citizens will take up grass-roots activism in growing numbers: They are learning about social action; they are becoming more and more aware of ethnic identities and class distinctions; and they have been invited to take active part in Project Renewal, the joint effort by the government and supporters in the Diaspora to rehabilitate Israel's worst slums.

A generation of Israelis has been taught by the media how to influence the allocation of services and resources. When television dramatizes pressure-group tactics and successes -- Georgian Jews demonstrating en masse for jobs at the port of Ashdod, or Gush Emunim winning new settlements, or labor unions and farmers demonstrating for wage and price supports, or couples sitting in for housing -- young Israelis learn that activism is a good way to make oneself heard. These media messages, seen hundreds of times, from early childhood on, and augmented by what youngsters hear in school about the justice and the how-to of teachers' strikes, add up to a powerful socialization process in favor of social action.

As economic, social and environmental problems have grown more acute, ideas on how to meet them have also changed. Most people realize that there will be no more government "handouts," as there were during the days of mass immigration; they now believe each person has to pull his or her own weight. But second-generation Israelis also feel that many of their problems are not of their own making, and that they need not suffer in silence when the load gets too heavy. They accordingly join to impress the authorities, municipal and national, with their grievances: overcrowded or run-down housing, lack of neighborhood amenities, the high cost of basic social services like day care or medical care, inadequate transportation, unfulfilled civil rights, too little education, religious controversies, not being heard in local or national affairs and so on.

Increased awareness of ethnic identities and class distinctions has led many Jews from Moslem countries to social activism, and the trend seems certain to continue at an even faster pace (Heller, 1973; Smooha, 1978). When Sephardi members of the Knesset talk about organizing a lobby that is to cut across the various parties, they may just be talking for the record, for political leaders will not as a rule jeopardize their party's support or their own careers through unsanctioned activities. But when Sephardi <u>landsmannschaften</u> flourish and take up social action alongside their traditional forms of self-help, it means something.

In this decade, increasing funds for militant action will probably come from wealthy Sephardim abroad who are disillusioned about the opportunities or non-opportunities offered to their brothers in Israel by what they see as a paternalistic Ashkenazi leadership. No longer content just to collect money for university scholarships, Sephardim may well assault the universities' admissions policies. Even though research studies have consistently shown that Sephardim in Israel identify strongly with Ashkenazi culture and lifestyle (Jaffe, 1980b), there are now clear signs of a Sephardi reawakening, of a proud Sephardi subculture in the making.

Rising expectations, particularly those aroused by Project Renewal, have been another source of growing discontent. A great deal of money ($1.2 billion) will be available for Project Renewal, and there is hope that things will really change. The project has a number of new wrinkles, such as integration of social and physical planning and the "twinning" of slum areas with Jewish communities abroad, but the most conspicuous innovation is the rule that slum residents are to have a voice in planning for their neighborhoods.

Thanks to this rule, indigenous leaders have been catapulted into partnership with City Hall and Diaspora leaders, and are suddenly holding key positions on steering committees. Slum dwellers have found out that neighborhood organization and advocacy can go far in influencing renewal plans and in giving local leaders a power base. The more sophisticated leaders have learned to build strong coalitions with participating Diaspora communities, which contribute 50 percent of Project Renewal's funds and can bring neighborhood spokesmen into the mayor's office through the front door. Many are studying English in order to communicate with "their" Federation leaders. They have also learned how to work through the press, deftly use the microphones at meetings of the Jewish Agency Assembly and other international Jewish bodies -- and are sure to pursue their course with even more determination in years to come.

Tougher Social Action

Judging by developments to date, social-action groups from the lower income levels will go in even more for confrontations and disruptive activities during the 1980s than heretofore, and will show even less patience for mere "warning" tactics and for the reliance on political processes which pressure groups from the less oppressed middle class prefer. On the other hand, at least some of the experienced, recognized leaders now emerging in lower-class pressure groups will undoubtedly be co-opted into the existing political framework and more or less neutralized.

For example, grass-roots leaders may be sidelined through the familiar ploy of "individual rehabilitation," i. e., by being offered jobs or apartments. This is what happened recently to a leader in Katamon, a Jerusalem slum: When he was helped to acquire an apartment in a suburb, his credibility and his accreditation as a representative of the old neighborhood in which he had grown up were instantly destroyed. The offers made in such cases are hard for anyone to turn down, especially someone from a disadvantaged background. Some think they can swallow the bait and then make the political parties work for them, but in the long run few can resist party discipline. You can raise an issue in the party and make your case, but if your view loses in the voting, you must support the party line.

The most remarkable development of the 1970s has been

the politicization of disadvantaged groups, particularly street-corner gangs. Earlier, these groups were simply training grounds for delinquency and antisocial behavior. Social workers would try to infiltrate them, diagnose the youngsters' problems, rehabilitate them one by one, and thus ultimately destroy the group. All that changed, however, when the Black Panthers turned themselves into a social-action group, formally disavowing delinquent activity and pledging themselves to work within the law for their neighborhood, as well as for disadvantaged Sephardi Jews throughout Israel.

Five years later, a street gang in Katamon, with help from Dr. Louis Miller, senior social psychiatrist at the Ministry of Health, and from other prominent Ashkenazi professionals, immersed itself in "street theater" under the name "Ohel Yosef Theatre Group." The members wrote their own plays and after each performance engaged the audience in dialogue with no holds barred -- an exercise in communication and catharsis, which enabled them to voice their protests effectively, bolstered their self-image and gave them confidence in their ability to debate and arouse interest. But after a while the catharsis wore off and left the neighborhood pretty much as it had always been. At this point, the group turned to lobbying and political activism.

In its new incarnation, Ohel Yosef became the first in a chain of neighborhood-based, grass-roots social groups. Within two years, six other <u>ohalim</u> or neighborhood roof organizations were organized in poor sections of Jerusalem, usually around a core of intelligent, highly motivated Sephardi ex-delinquents. The bulk of social workers and community organizers have not yet learned just how to handle this new kind of organization, and in any case, as noted earlier, their employers are wary of letting them get too involved in political activity. But with or without professional help, the politicization of street-corner gangs bids fair to spread across the nation.

As grass-roots groups, the <u>ohalim</u> are entitled to participate in neighborhood steering committees for Project Renewal, and this has given them a major impetus. At the same time, the World Sephardi Federation has begun to grant them some limited funding (limited in comparison with what it could give), thereby laying the groundwork for a partnership which could become highly significant if it develops more fully and if the <u>ohalim</u> are up to the task.

There have been occasional relapses into delinquency.

On one occasion, Panthers stole milk containers in Rehavia,
a well-to-do neighborhood, and left them on doorsteps in
the Asbestos slum; on another, ohalim members burned
tires during a protest against steep food-price rises
and the lifting of subsidies on basic foods, and got into
a fight with the police. For all that, the trend toward
politicization of street-corner gangs is clearly healthy
and should be encouraged.

Grass-roots Groups vs. Government

As neighborhood and grass-roots groups begin to represent themselves, the role of civil servants who advocate central planning over local action is called into question. The record shows why: In undertakings like Project Renewal, most of the significant progress takes place in neighborhood steering committees; most of the exasperating bottlenecks occur in the Ministries and the Jewish Agency in Jerusalem, with their bureaucratic and political hassles.

Grass-roots and social-action groups have become wary of civil servants who offer paternalistic aid. Their suspicion extends even to social workers and community organizers, who are thus caught in the crossfire between their clients and their employers. Out of loyalty to citizen groups, some organizers have developed elaborate under-the-table tactics and "dirty games": leaking surveys and reports of scandalous conditions to the media, consulting about confrontation methods, even participating in rallies and demonstrations. But these are the exceptions; by and large, "establishment" workers encounter growing antagonism among the underprivileged.

The social-work profession clearly is not a major partner in citizens' social-action programs now, and probably never will be. It is not committed to altering political and social institutions, for all that some of its members are reformers or radicals. In Israel, schools of social work do not offer instruction in social-action skills and methods (where do they?), and when they profess to encourage student involvement in social-action programs, it is mostly window-dressing. Teaching such skills would be difficult at best, because there is no coherent body of knowledge about the subject; it would bring no academic kudos, and its net effect might merely be to turn social workers into perennial caretakers of client groups. Most important, the school that undertakes to train future public servants in this explosive subject would probably bring political or economic sanctions, possibly lethal ones, upon itself and career retaliation upon the teachers.

As taught in Israeli universities during the next decade, "community organization," so-called, will mean social planning, social policy, social administration and theory of social change -- none of them of much use to social-action groups. Some day, perhaps, private funding will fill the gap by offering special courses to neighborhood leaders, or by giving grass-roots citizen organizations money to hire professional community workers on their own, as some churches in the United States have done to help disadvantaged minority groups. Perhaps philanthropists abroad could become interested in such a scheme for Israel?

The Future of Volunteerism

Volunteerism, in the sense of providing manpower for existing services and agencies, may be in for hard times in Israel. As inflation continues unabated, fed by uncontrollable energy prices, many Israelis may decide to devote their spare time to earning additional income. Volunteer work may thus become largely the province of the well-to-do, of older, retired people and of school-age youngsters enlisted through quasi-mandatory school programs or ad hoc youth movement activities. If so, volunteering is bound to become less spontaneous and less indigenous. A renewed awareness of social problems and a broader sense of a common cause might conceivably offset this trend, but perhaps only the threat of catastrophe -- for example, a new military crisis -- could prompt such a reawakening.

Certain forms of volunteering may remain relatively stable: adopting army units, other activities related to defense and the armed forces, helping with health care and perhaps founding or aiding new settlements. Others, like tutoring and face-to-face help to welfare clients, may suffer badly. If so, the welfare establishment -- the Ministry of Labor and Social Affairs and the municipalities -- may be forced to develop new paraprofessional roles or expand existing ones, in order to take the pressure off overworked staff without the expense of hiring additional social workers. Such a move would undoubtedly encounter stiff resistance by the Israel Association of Social Workers, which has fought for two decades to get social work recognized as an academic profession and to keep its functions and status from being watered down. Today, about 3,500 of Israel's 4,500 social workers are graduates of professional schools, and efforts are afoot to reduce the number of nonprofessionals. Legislation to require licensing of social workers is pending in the Knesset.

Since it is likely that grass-roots citizen groups will proliferate in the new decade and turn into powerful political and social-action enterprises, while volunteering and the importance of professional community organizers decline, it may be helpful to take a close look at the history and prospects of one relatively old grass-roots organization now undergoing this development. The organization is Zahavi, the Israeli Association for Rights of Large Families. Its story will be told in the first person by one who was there.

ZAHAVI: ANATOMY OF A GRASS-ROOTS ORGANIZATION

Few people outside Israel have heard of Zahavi, Israel's association for large families ("large" meaning "with four or more children"), but Israelis have watched this grass-roots group with keen interest since it began. I do not find it easy to describe Zahavi objectively, having been one of its founders. But perhaps only an eyewitness who is also a social scientist could write the full story, with all the revealing bits of inside information.

Origins

In 1972, when I was rounding out a two-year stint as director of Jerusalem's Department of Family and Community Services, a stranger walked in with a dream. Avraham Danino, 45, born in Morocco and living in Israel since 1948, proposed an association that would press for the rights of Israel's 80,000 large families without relying on professional or political intermediaries. A former city councilman in Haifa, currently supervisor of a government program for disadvantaged youth, Danino had become disillusioned with the deadening co-optation of ethnic leaders by political parties. He was convinced that the country needed independent groups to work for social change.

As it happened, I had arrived at the same conclusion by another route. In years of research at the Hebrew University, I and my students had found the existing welfare system faultily conceptualized, paternalistic and incapable of helping the poor gain self-esteem or overcome dependency. I thought policy-makers would listen if welfare recipients were to speak up for themselves, but no welfare-rights movement had ever gotten off the ground, because self-images were too poor and leaders too scarce. Even the Black Panthers, whose leaders could not be co-opted or bought off with seductive job offers or ad hoc local programs, had -- like most other protest movements -- been unsuccessful in building a mass organization.

My own involvement with the Black Panthers was still fresh in my mind the day I met Danino. I had counseled the Mayor to talk to the Panthers and help them get a permit to demonstrate, but like most politicians at the time -- none of whom would admit it today -- he was frightened by the Panthers and would have no part of them. He was convinced that they were an "American import," created by me and my workers. (I had immigrated to Israel from the U. S. 12 years earlier.) Yet the Panthers, through their discovery of "two Israels," one rich and one poor, had subsequently sparked some changes, not all of them just token changes, in the Government's attitude toward the underclass. As much as anything, this sequence of events convinced me that there was no chance of significant social change without sophisticated, independent grass-roots organizations.

Danino and I almost immediately found each other on the same wave length concerning family size. Both he and I had come from large families and were fathers of large families. Both of us knew that 10 percent of Israel's families were producing more than 40 percent of her children, and that nearly every other Israeli soldier came from a large family. But we also knew that such families were hit harder than others by inflation, cuts in food subsidies, overcrowded housing and heavy taxes, and we were indignant that they were shown so little respect.

The family as an institution, of whatever size, has taken a beating in the modern, quasi-socialist, Western-minded Israel created by Europeans and children of Europeans. Kibbutz living, which has greatly influenced attitudes even though only 3 percent of the people now live on kibbutzim, has also tended to reduce the size and importance of families. The Government has no clear policy on family size, even though the birthrate of Jews has sharply declined in comparison with that of Moslems, largely because of the rapid Westernization of many Sephardi families (Schmelz, 1976).

The public's attitude toward large families is predominantly negative. A majority of Israelis will concede that the country needs higher birthrates -- often referred to as "internal immigration" -- needs more people to defend itself; at the same time, there is a tendency to condemn people with large families as shiftless and stupid, or as irresponsible parasites and breeders of delinquents -- in short as "undeserving poor." Since most big families are either Middle-Eastern Sephardim or (less often) Orthodox Ashkenazim, those stereotypes also have ugly ethnic and religious components.

Thus Danino and I saw two challenges ahead. One was to gain respect and obtain help for the despised big families -- a task which such families themselves, once organized, probably could handle better than even the most skilled social workers and most liberal politicians, who would be vulnerable to all sorts of pressures. The other challenge was to awaken the rest of the nation to the option of raising large families, for the sake of Israel's future, to replace part of the six million lost in our lifetime, and for the joy of raising children.

And so Zahavi was born. The name, invented by Danino, is an acronym for Zechuyot Hamishpachot Bruchot Yeladim, "Association for the Rights of Families Blessed with Children," but it also means "my gold," for the organization's guiding belief was to be that Israel's real treasure was her children.

Growing Pains

Zahavi was incorporated as a nonprofit organization on April 17, 1972, and subsequently established tax-exempt status. The incorporators were Avraham Danino, Amiram Harlap, a Haifa lawyer; Leon Madgar, a professor at the Technion; Meri Levi, a Moshav Yesharesh founder; Rabbi Simcha Hacohen Kook, the Chief Rabbi of Rehovot; Shmuel Chayoun, a Haifa businessman; Dr. Eugene Wiener of Haifa University, and myself. Zahavi was to be independent of any and all political parties and government agencies. Its goals were defined as follows:

1. To create a positive public attitude toward families blessed with many children.

2. To promote creation of a network of services that would enable large families to live with dignity.

3. To foster legislation for the welfare of large families, including revision of local and national tax laws, as well as guarantees to mothers of large families of all rights now enjoyed by women working outside the home.

4. To increase the purchasing power of large families through special reductions in the price of goods and services, whether supplied by government or the private sector.

5. To provide counseling and other services that would enable large families to make a contribution to society.

Under Zahavi's constitution, branches send elected representatives to a National Council. The Council in turn chooses the national officers, who make up the National Executive Committee. In the branches, the members elect local executive committees. (As things have developed, the committees of branches in the smaller towns sometimes comprise almost the whole active membership.)

Zahavi went to work the moment it was incorporated, lobbying vigorously for needed legislation. Simultaneously, bylaws had to be drafted, national branch committees organized, financial responsibilities assigned and a hundred other chores seen to as part of completing the transition from a cluster of freewheeling individuals to a properly organized national association.

As Zahavi made news and grew, volunteers spent longer and longer hours on the road and at late evening meetings, helping set up branches and advising them. More often than

not, they paid the expenses out of their own pockets. By
1977 the job had become unmanageable, and Zahavi asked the
Ministry of Labor and Social Affairs for a grant to hire
community organizers. The Ministry hesitated; until then it
had budgeted funds only for strictly welfare purposes and
here was a group that was not uniformly poor, though largely
so. In the end, however, the Minister gave the request
his personal blessing.

Two early friends of Zahavi were Israel Katz, Minister
of Labor and Social Affairs, and Deputy Prime Minister
Yigal Yadin. Their publicly avowed interest greatly
helped the organization gain status in the eyes of the public.
Minister Katz also helped finance a mail campaign in 1977,
which in three weeks brought in more than 8,000 new member-
ships.

Today, thanks almost entirely to volunteer efforts,
Zahavi has over 20,000 member families. They come from widely
differing socio-economic strata and ethnic groups; over 85
percent are of Sephardi origin. Branches now number 24 and
reach from Maalot, near the Lebanese border, to Kiryat Arba
(Hebron) in Judea, the largest being those in Haifa, the
Tel Aviv-Holon area and Jerusalem. Morale is high; most
members are active and strongly motivated, and shared interests have made for exceptionally good relations between the
varied social and ethnic groups that constitute this
microcosm of Israel.

Legislative Efforts

Promoting legislation that will help large families,
and opposing measures that will hurt them, has been Zahavi's
chief activity to date, ahead even of fostering self-help
and changing imagery. When a pertinent bill is before the
Knesset, Zahavi may testify in committee hearings, often
with elaborate position papers or statistical exhibits,
or call privately on Knesset members and political officials,
or alert the public through press conferences or rallies.
In 1979, the Knesset gave official recognition of a sort to
Zahavi's activities by presenting the head of the organization
with a permanent admission pass and a space in the official
parking lot.

Whenever possible, Zahavi works in tandem with organizations and agencies that share its concerns. Among its coalition partners are the Ministry of Labor and Social Affairs
and the National Insurance Institute, Israel's social security
agency. (In 1979, Zahavi organized a protest by some 6,000
families to back the Insurance Institute's opposition to cuts
in social insurance proposed by the Finance Ministry.) At
the same time, Zahavi, as a wholly independent organization,
can speak out promptly and unreservedly through the mass

media when the rights of large families are endangered.

Zahavi was crucial in staving off the worst proposed cuts in children's allowances; in reducing water rates charged to large families; in getting the mothers the tax advantage of working-mother status, and in raising their subsidies by 150 Israel pounds semi-annually, which increased the collective income of these families by 20 million pounds a year. In a number of towns, Zahavi won big reductions in nursery-school tuition, fees for summer recreation programs and admission to municipal theaters.

When subsidies on basic commodities were repeatedly cut during the Rabin and Begin administrations, Zahavi joined with the National Insurance Institute, Histradrut and the Israel Association of Social Workers to see that large families were promptly and equitably compensated. After the newly elected Begin government made its first cuts, members of the Alignment-Labor opposition, urgently in need of weapons for a countermove, called on Zahavi as the best source of information on what the cuts were doing to large families. They had learned to respect Zahavi's expertise when <u>they</u> were in the saddle.

Zahavi was the prime mover in putting a free high school education within the reach of every youngster in Israel. The idea, as submitted to the Minister of Education, was to meet the cost through a modest standardized deduction from all wages, so that all members of one generation would pay for the next. Parents would no longer be charged tuition, scaled by income, for 11th-and 12th-grade students; they would be freed from a degrading means test and a financial burden greater than that of sending a son or daughter to college. The army of clerks and financial investigators that had managed the old system could be disbanded.

The plan was opposed by some who did not want to give free education to the rich. Zahavi's answer was that the progressive income tax already kept the well-to-do from getting too much of a free ride. More serious was a disagreement with the leading women's organizations (which operate most of Israel's day-care centers): Women's International Zionist Organization, Pioneer Women and Mizrachi Women. These three formed a powerful lobby for universal free day care, which Zahavi intended to join once free high schools were attained; but the women's groups wanted free day care even before free high schools. Free high schools were introduced in September, 1979; Zahavi will join the coalition to secure free day care in the coming years.

Inevitably, Zahavi has had its share of failures and bogged-down efforts. One of its thornier undertakings has been a proposal of a "Magna Carta for large families": a measure that would anchor in one law all rights and entitlements of big families in housing, education and other fields. A group of lawyers who were Zahavi members drafted a bill; other members, sitting at street-corner tables, collected 30,000 signatures, which were sent with maximum fanfare to President Katzir and Prime Minister Begin.

Unfortunately, the proposal soon became a political football. While the ruling Alignment hesitated, the Likud opposition pounced on the bill, hoping to seize the initiative in social legislation and embarrass the other side. With Zahavi's help, endorsements from 52 Knesset members, including Menahem Begin and Simcha Ehrlich, were quickly obtained. But just as quickly, the Alignment washed its hands of what had become an obvious partisan maneuver.

When Likud became the governing party, the Alignment in turn resurrected the bill. With 14 endorsements from Alignment members and 34 from Likud and other parties, prospects seemed bright, especially as Mr. Ehrlich, now Finance Minister, reaffirmed his support and even set up a committee to explore the implementation of the proposed law. But now Yigal Yadin sidetracked the bill into the Interministerial Conference on Social Welfare, of which he was chairman. And there it sits, despite all attempts to pry it loose.

Also still on Zahavi's agenda is a proposed law under which all property taxes would be assessed according to family size, not family income. (Meanwhile, Zahavi branches in 12 cities have pushed through local ordinances to that effect.) A bill making Zahavi the sole legal representative of large families is also hanging fire. The law would require legislators to consult Zahavi on legislation affecting large families. It would also make the National Insurance roster of large families public and provide Zahavi with a complete mailing list and government postal privileges, facilitating the recruitment of new members to increase the organization's political power and add to its skimpy funds. Zahavi will continue to fight for this measure, even if it means going to court.

Self-help and Service Projects

What kinds of projects and services Zahavi should offer to members has often been debated, but there is no unanimity. Some branches believe they can be most useful by arranging loans, or by helping families save money (for example, by making surplus foodstuffs available at big discounts). Others think this kind of assistance smacks too much of welfare and dependency, and consider it preferable by far to undertake programs whose emphasis is on self-help.

Lack of capital rather than of ideas has limited the development of projects. Thus the Jerusalem branch decided to open a second-hand furniture exchange and secured a grant of 100,000 Israel pounds from the National Insurance Institute. But the branch could never raise the additional 200,000 pounds required, and in the end, sadly, returned the seed money.

At least one of Zahavi's aid projects came into being through what seems like the hand of fate. A party of Protestant tourists from Switzerland woke up one morning to learn that the Yom Kippur War had begun. Spontaneously, the visitors vowed to do something concrete for Israel's future. Out of this vow came Zahavi's "S.O.S. Scholarship Fund" for children of large families who have dropped out of school, or are about to, for lack of tutorial help or other reasons. Without much fanfare, the Swiss group has channeled over a million pounds to the fund, with gratifying results.

Zahavi's Schoolbook Library Project has helped hundreds, and eventually will help thousands, of large disadvantaged families obtain a home library of basic texts and reference works. A typical library costs about $250, 40 percent of which is covered by a publisher's discount, and another 40 percent by Zahavi. (In some localities, the mayor provides matching funds for Zahavi's share.) The remaining 20 percent is paid by the family, so that any suggestion of a handout is avoided. The books are selected to help children of all ages do their homework properly, and some of the more permanent, such as atlases and encyclopedias, may even last to serve the next generation. It is not easy to describe the faces of children and parents when they receive their books.

Legal aid for large families was introduced by Zahavi several years ago, made possible by the generosity of a long-time friend in the United States. Many public services in Israel are not anchored in specific laws but in administrative directives and regulations, so that there is much latitude for decisions by the bureaucracy. Zahavi believes that the terms of key regulations affecting disadvantaged families in the areas of housing, health and welfare need to be more sharply defined and clarified by court decisions. Hence the Legal Aid Project, under which Zahavi represents families in class actions and other precedent-setting cases. Each year several carefully selected cases are brought, the best lawyers retained and the legal costs paid. Often the mere threat of legal proceedings is enough; in most cases, the agencies concerned have settled out of court. In one case, in 1980, an injunction was obtained from the Supreme Court, setting a precedent for slum renewal in Israel.

Projects under discussion include food co-ops, family counseling and special publications addressed to large families. However, there is some risk that expansion of self-help and service projects may siphon off too much volunteer (and eventually, employee) manpower from equally necessary social-action and lobbying functions. Whether the organization will be able to do justice to both types of activities is one of the more worrisome questions ahead.

Moments of Decision

Like every other organization that gains public recognition, Zahavi has faced moral dilemmas and political risks. Take, for example, the case of Flatto Sharon, a multimillionaire who was wanted in France for alleged fraud and gained immunity from extradition when he was elected to the Knesset. Before his election, in what was clearly a bid for endorsement, he professed to be interested in Zahavi; afterwards, still in search of a power base and a positive image, he suggested various ways in which he might aid the organization, such as setting up discount stores for large families. In return he wanted the exclusive right to lobby on Zahavi's behalf in the Knesset for a period of six months, plus a seat on the Executive Council.

Though the promises of material and political support were tempting, Zahavi did not give Mr. Sharon the endorsement he wanted, nor did it agree to the deal he later proposed. His demands were found unacceptable, and his plans for aiding Zahavi remained vague. Most important, association with so controversial a figure seemed likely to cast doubt on Zahavi's integrity and independence. And so, after repeated long debates, the flirtation came to an end.

A fateful decision of another kind had to be made when Prime Minister Rabin resigned and called new elections. Many members wanted to run one or several candidates for the Knesset, who, if elected, could be counted on to introduce bills the association wanted. Pros and cons were intensely argued in the branches, at a national rally and in the National Council. It was finally decided that Zahavi would not run as a party, so as not to endanger its appeal among the constituents, who belonged to many different parties, but that individual members could run in any party they chose. Thus Zahavi did not go the route of the Black Panthers, and few today regret that decision.

In 1979, a crucial question with which Zahavi had wrestled for years came to a head: Should Israelis who were not Jews be admitted to membership, even though the Moslems were in no danger of population loss? The debate in the National Council was loud and bitter. In the end, a majority voted to let Arabs join and to steer Zahavi toward becoming a truly national lobby for all large families in the country. Coupled with this decision, however, was a resolution to press for a law that would make some form of national service compulsory for all Israelis, including Arabs. If there were to be equality between Arabs and Jews, it was felt, it would have to mean equality in all aspects of life (Geiger, 1979).

Most of Zahavi's membership can no doubt live with these decisions. They are not likely to change Zahavi's overwhelmingly Jewish makeup very much, if only because potential Arab members will look with less than enchantment upon an organization that advocates a compulsory national service law. But at least the issues have been clarified for the time being.

Overseas Relations and Funding

Up to now, Zahavi's work has been almost entirely Israel-based. In 1973, the association called for support from Diaspora Jews and found a few sympathizers in the U.S., who raised a modest amount of money, sent out some publicity and obtained tax-exempt status for donations made in the U.S. Most U.S. donations have been given to the Israel Endowment Fund (P.E.F.) in New York and earmarked for specific non-political self-help projects of Zahavi. Since 1977 somewhat more volunteer effort has been forthcoming, but even now there are no strong ties to like-minded groups abroad.

From time to time, individuals in the Diaspora recognize the significance of Zahavi's work, and meeting with these is always sheer joy. Take, for example, Sam Jacobson of Halifax, Nova Scotia. In 1976, Mr. Jacobson, retired and a man of means, read an article on "The Jewish Right to Multiply" in the overseas edition of the Jerusalem Post and wrote Zahavi a note of congratulations. A little later a donation followed, and after another three months he turned up in Jerusalem to see for himself.

Avraham Danino came from Haifa to talk to him. Mr. Jacobson added some angles of his own, and from then on there was no holding him. His energy was the envy of Zahavi's far younger leaders. He made a sizable grant to Zahavi, on condition that the organization run a series of one-inch ads with slogans in two weekend newspapers until a designated amount of money ran out. (Sample ad: "Not charity or handouts, but a declaration of rights for large families!" The ads did not raise much money, but were seen by huge numbers of readers and did a great deal to make Zahavi known and understood. They also prompted the Israel radio to do a ten-minute program, which received excellent feedback.

Mr. Jacobson eventually parted ways with Zahavi, because the organization did not choose to follow his suggestion that it devote itself entirely to the anti-abortion cause. But his help is unforgotten, as is the friendship of others -- such as the shy, motherly psychologist and businesswoman from Switzerland, who helped prepare and pay for the printing of Zahavi's first brochures and its national newsletter. Or the young American who owned stadium concessions and a football team and came to Jerusalem asking what he could do to help. In the never-ending job of building support, the human contacts have been as interesting and rewarding as the work itself.

The Next Few Years

Israel does not treat grass-roots citizen organizations with much tenderness. Few have surmounted the political and financial barriers in their way. In my opinion, Zahavi has "taken off": It has demonstrated its usefulness and gained a role in Israeli society. But it is not yet making the most of its role.

Zahavi began as a purely volunteer organization. Its early efforts depended on a small core of active individuals around the country, all volunteering in their various areas of expertise and interest. Danino and a handful of others pulled these efforts together into an organized whole, with considerable success in both lobbying and self-help projects. Now the work load, the membership and the challenges have increased to a point where carefully selected paid employees are needed if the members are not to be seriously frustrated.

One danger the movement faces is its own tendency toward centralization. In the past, a degree of centralization was necessary to facilitate action on national issues. By this time, however, a good many talented local leaders have emerged in the branches, and they must take on greater responsibilities. Zahavi's success to date is largely the result of Avraham Danino's charismatic leadership, but for the organizational tasks that lie ahead charisma is not enough.

I can testify that Danino himself foresaw this development as early as 1973, during the Yom Kippur War. As I learned on returning from extended reserve duty, his oldest son, Moshe, was missing in action on the Egyptian front. For weeks, Danino and his family went from hospital to hospital, searching for army comrades who might know about Moshe. Finally their worst fears were confirmed. I visited Avraham, his wife Rina and their other children while they were sitting shiva, and Avraham said to me, using his favorite metaphor for raising children: "We've been busy growing our own flowers. Now we must help other people grow theirs. And that is more than a one-man job."

Zahavi has become too potent to function merely on an ad hoc basis. It has been tested and found effective -- more so than could have been foreseen. With adequate funding and full-time manpower, it could become one of the most significant citizens'-rights and self-help groups in Israel. It cuts across the differences in ethnicity, color, politics and religion that often divide Israelis. It speaks to the continuity and quality of the Jewish people and Jewish family life in Israel.

And not only in Israel. For some time, sympathizers in the U. S. and elsewhere have wanted Zahavi to become an international movement with branches in different countries, dedicated to overcoming Jewry's present state of virtually zero population growth. The means are not yet in sight, but it is possible that an international organization will be launched at a World Convention on Large Families, which Zahavi hopes to convene in Jerusalem in a few years. It will be interesting to see what the Zahavi experiment will mean, not only for the future of the Jewish State, but also for that of Jewry all over the world.

AGENDA FOR LEADERS

Having examined current trends in the different forms of citizen involvement in Israel, with their benefits and drawbacks, and having obtained a bird's-eye view of one grass-roots citizen group, what implications do we see for Israelis and for Diaspora Jews?

Lessons for Israelis
-

One important message to Israelis is that the time has come to recognize the limitations of "classic" volunteering and the legitimacy and potential power of social-action and grass-roots organizations. With new opportunities for citizen activity at hand, individuals need to reassess how they can make the most of their time, energy and resources. "Classic" volunteering may well prove less rewarding than other modes of involvement.

It certainly is not too early for privately sponsored leadership programs to train adults and young people in methods of advocacy and neighborhood organization. One such program, funded by the Jewish Agency, was recently conducted by that organization's Department of Sephardi Communities in cooperation with the Hebrew University's Program for Community Leadership, the Jerusalem Municipality's Public Relations and Welfare Departments and Histadrut's Jerusalem Worker's Council. Twenty neighborhood activists attended lectures on the following subjects:

1. The power of Israel's political institutions.

2. Public social services in neighborhoods.

3. How to reach the media.

4. Relationships between ministries and municipalities.

5. The power of the neighborhood among political forces, and the rules of the power game in neighborhoods.

6. Who makes policy at the neighborhood, municipal and national levels?

7. How to choose a method for formulating strategies.

8. Stages of planning strategy.

9. How to organize and activate neighborhood residents.

10. Types of organization: formal and informal.

11. How to express yourself to other people.

12. Social issues specific to Jerusalem.

13. Styles of leadership.

The sessions were held one evening a week. The participants were <u>ohalim</u>, Zahavi and Panther leaders, plus members of neighborhood area committees, Project Renewal steering committee members and emerging leaders of various groups. They were enthusiastic and highly motivated; attendance was steady. Ten years ago, this project would have been inconceivable, and no one would have funded it. Even now, many people find programs of this kind unnecessary or fear that they will incite neighborhood groups. But the fact remains that many disadvantaged groups are turning to social action, not volunteering, to change conditions.

A second message for Israelis is that social-action groups can work with government, national or local, to alter social conditions. True, politicians and bureaucrats are often afraid of social-action groups, and social activists often distrust politicians and bureaucrats. Yet the two groups have been known to cooperate successfully when their interests coincided, and on occasion public officials have emerged with their values thoroughly changed.

This happened, for example, to Shlomo ("Chich") Lahat, who campaigned his way from a high post in the Defense Forces into the mayoralty of Tel Aviv. In 1965, when he was Chief of the Manpower Division in the General Staff, I called on him to urge that the Army draft youngsters with minor criminal records, thus giving them a last chance to become productive citizens. But "Chich" said no -- the Army could not take problem kids, because they could not be trusted to be responsible for their comrades.

Fifteen years later, we met again: at a meeting of Welfare Federation leaders in Cleveland, Ohio, where I was to talk about Project Renewal and "Chich" was to appear on behalf of a run-down Tel Aviv neighborhood, which under Project Renewal was "twinned" with Cleveland. By this time he had been mayor for two years and had learned something about social issues. After I spoke, he followed with a moving, incisive talk about his city's human problems, stressing particularly that more young Israelis must be helped to become involved in improving their society. A real metamorphosis!

Israeli community-organization workers must be prepared for increased pressures from the municipalities that employ them and from neighborhood groups. Perhaps the idea that social activism could be a major part of community organizers' professional education or their work was an illusion, nurtured by social-work professionals and educators. Community workers will be able to get intimately involved in social action only when they are hired to do so by non-governmental organizations with access to private funds -- whenever that day comes.

The capacity and need of Israelis to take active part in the affairs of the country should not be underestimated. Few nations' citizens have risen so many times to so many challenges. The full wealth of Israel's human resources is still untapped and unmeasured, but it is available to those who know where to find it. While compiling a <u>Directory of Non-Profit, Volunteer Organizations in Israel</u>, I have thus far found over 3,000 such groups, and there probably are many more. Israelis must do everything possible to encourage this kind of civic effort.

Diaspora Support for Israel

Jews in the Diaspora will undoubtedly continue to play a crucial role in helping Israel grapple with her social problems. This may entail certain new departures in philanthropy, for, paradoxical as it may sound, there is some reason to believe that the mechanisms through which organized world Jewry aids Israel have to some degree stifled Israeli initiative and hindered the formation of close relationships between Israelis and Jews in other lands.

Most of the funds raised for Israel abroad -- through the United Jewish Appeal, Keren Hayesod and Israel Bonds -- are channelled through governmental and quasi-governmental agencies into ongoing services and projects. In the lively competition for these funds, government ministries and municipalities hold many more cards than do private, volunteer citizen groups -- for one thing because it is easier for the Diaspora to deal with one recipient than with hundreds. This system of allocation has worked fairly well for three decades, but in recent years some negative by-products have become evident.

With or without the Government's blessing, a large network of private, non-profit social services has grown up in Israel. Women's groups, from Hadassah to Mizrachi Women, have developed their own fund-raising constituencies abroad,

while also lobbying vigorously for government money, and
groups like Keren Yaldenu, Habad, Alin, Akim and hundreds
of other non-profit volunteer service organizations have
fought their way onto the welfare scene by the same route.
Still other hundreds of welfare enterprises and ideas, however, have failed the fund-raising test.

It might be argued that this is the normal process of
"survival of the fittest." But were the causes that were
vanquished in the contest necessarily unfit? In all probability, a good many potentially useful services did not get off
the ground simply for lack of seed money or experience, and
a good many innovative ideas from the grass roots were stillborn because they were contrary to Establishment thinking
or too independent of government control. It is for
reasons like these that Israel still has no private, non-profit legal aid for the disadvantaged, no private, non-profit adoption or foster-care agencies, no strong civil-rights organization and few significant citizens' lobbies
concerned with welfare services.

American fund raising for Israel consists, as I once
put it, of "chore and shnorr": of responding to the United
Jewish Appeal and aiding the "independents." The UJA effort tends to present Israel's welfare needs in stereotyped group terms like "the aged," "the poor" or "the
children," without explaining just what people are included in these categories or what their needs are. For
many American Jews, giving for Israel has become mechanical,
a means to gain status in the local community rather than to
build a partnership between themselves and the Israelis.

Perhaps Israel's need for resources and Diaspora
Jewry's recognized or unrecognized need for a less impersonal donor relationship with Israel could both be met by
institutionalizing independent gifts to philanthropic
causes in a fixed ratio to a donor's other contributions.
To make the idea palatable to existing fund-raising organizations, the independent gift could be added "at the top,"
as an extra percentage above the "regular" donation. For
example, the ratio could be set at 10 to 1, so that a
donor who gives $2,000 a year to the UJA would give $200 a
year to an Israeli organization of his own choice.

Whether by this method or another, we must somehow reduce the power of government to decide single-handedly
which causes are acceptable and which are not, and we must
find a way to open up honorable, professional competition
in Israel for private welfare dollars from abroad.

For those who are thinking of making independent grants

to welfare programs in Israel, here are a few suggested rules:

1. Do not support programs in Israel that you would not support elsewhere. For example, orphanages and institutions for babies are out everywhere. Ask a social-service expert in your country whether the project you are considering is sound in principle, then find out just how it is to be implemented.

2. When you give money, insist on periodic accounting and professional evaluation of the program. Don't settle for pictures of smiling children or tear-jerker success stories.

3. Do not get involved in raising money on an ongoing basis if you have no say about how it is spent. Any organization that asks your support owes you a detailed description of how funds are to be allocated and a hearing for your comments. Insist on it, even at the risk that the organization may disagree with your views and decline your money.

4. Stay away from any program that should be a responsibility of the Israeli Government, unless it is a demonstration project to catalyze government agencies into action.

5. Avoid programs no longer in tune with Israel's changing needs. Choose innovative projects. Have the nerve to support ideas that may be unpopular at City Hall but are popular with grass-roots sponsors.

6. Do not shy away from social-action and advocacy ventures, particularly if they hold a promise of influencing legislation, nationally or locally. Always ask yourself what the influence of a particular project will be five or ten years hence. Are new policies or services likely to spin off from the effort? Or will it be just hit-and-run?

7. Do your homework. Never give money without informing yourself about issues and controversies in the area concerned, and about the way social work is conducted there. Ask your Federation or your relatives in Israel to help check facts. Write to social-service practitioners in Israel for information and for the names of others who might help. If you plan to visit Israel, set aside a few days to look at potential projects.

8. Take your philanthropy seriously. Don't apologize for asking questions; be tough-minded about investing in welfare enterprises. Think of yourself as a partner in the project, not a casual benefactor.

9. Remember that the worth of the cause you support cannot always be judged by the number or the status of the friends you make. On the contrary, you can sometimes judge success by listing the people you upset by your efforts.

Face to Face

Over and above devising new ways of raising money for Israel's struggle against her social problems, Diaspora Jews should strive to become involved in the struggle itself. They can, for example, seek out face-to-face encounters with those who live in the midst of it, as social workers or clients. They can acquaint themselves with social-service institutions and programs. They can urge their Jewish communities back home to "twin" themselves with neighborhoods in Israel. And they can organize service programs in Israel for volunteers -- young people, adults or whole families -- from abroad.

As yet, volunteering does not figure on the agenda of most youth or adult groups visiting Israel. The visitors usually go on outings and attend educational seminars in relative isolation from the Israeli public. Foreigners interested in volunteer work almost always gravitate to the kibbutzim, which have developed a convenient work-for-lodging arrangement.

Using foreign volunteers in social services would be much more difficult than using them on the kibbutz -- if only because they would have to know at least some Hebrew, stay for a fairly long time and accept professional supervision. Still, a successful attempt, small in scale but sophisticated in style, has been made by the Jewish Agency in its Sherut La'am Program for young adults. Conceivably, the relationships now being forged by Project Renewal may give rise to enough interest and even elicit sufficient funds to try the idea on a large scale.

Since government agencies, understandably, are in no hurry to fund social-action groups and grass-roots community organizations, other financial resources will have to be found for them. Fortunately, such resources already exist in funds such as those of the UJA and Keren

Hayesod. This private wealth traditionally has been funneled into government-approved social enterprises, but there is no reason why some of it could not be used to support unconventional social movements and self-help organizations, even if their goal at times is to make government officials uncomfortable. UJA contributors and Diaspora leaders could give non-profit volunteer organizations in Israel a tremendous boost by insisting that the Jewish Agency and the Joint Distribution Committee make grants to them, subject to proper monitoring and accountability standards.

The ultimate form of participation in Israeli affairs is, of course, aliyah (immigration), for people remain Israel's greatest need. Unfortunately, most American Jews are quite ambivalent in their attitudes on this subject. They glow with pride at the thought that an American immigrant's son gave his life while leading the Entebbe raid; yet aliyah remains to them a conflict-ridden issue.

American community Federations will not endorse or subsidize programs to promote aliyah -- ostensibly because the donations they receive cannot legally be used for this purpose, actually because they are afraid of provoking ill will among non-Jews and opposition within the community. Individuals, including a good many members of women's Zionist organizations, worry about "losing" their children through aliyah. Rabbis and respected community leaders hardly ever advocate it, perhaps because they would feel hypocritical in recommending a move they themselves are not ready to make.

In the hope of modifying these attitudes, regional aliyah councils were set up in Cleveland, Detroit, Miami, New York and other places, in the wake of a National Aliyah Planning Conference, held in 1975. Since they have lacked both financial resources and broad community approval, the councils have not been particularly effective up to now in their objective. Properly funded, they could help meet the practical needs of American immigrants in Israel and could assign paid or unpaid liaison personnel to guide them through Israel's bureaucratic and legal mazes. They could also advise potential immigrants and even evaluate emissaries sent from Israel to promote aliyah. Jewish communities could join the effort -- for example, by offering loans, which could be turned into grants after the borrower had spent a specified number of years in Israel.

Functions like these should be of interest to American

Jewry as a whole, for "making aliyah" is not only the private act of an individual, but also a contribution by that individual's home community to the enrichment of the Jewish state. It would make sense to reserve some portion of the funds raised by Federations each year for the aliyah councils, thereby encouraging individuals and communities to make this contribution.

To institutionalize aid to persons "making aliyah" would be a significant change in communal priorities. It would take courage but it would be worth the risk. The resulting face-to-face encounters between Israelis and American Jews -- encounters likely to be more personal and meaningful than most of today's more or less anonymous fund-raising events -- might not be the smallest of the rewards.

Immigration is still Israel's lifeblood, no matter how much money is raised for the UJA.

BIBLIOGRAPHY

Amidar Corporation (1964). *Community Work in Israeli Housing Estates*, Report to the Twelfth International Conference of Social Work, Athens.

Cloward, Richard A., and Elman, M. (1970). "Advocacy in the Ghetto," in Cox, E., et al. (editors), *Strategies of Community Organizing*, Peacock Publishing Co., Itasca, Illinois.

Cromer, Gerald. (1976). "The Israeli Black Panthers: Fighting for Credibility and a Cause," *Victimology*, 1:3, 403-413.

Geiger, Aryeh. "One Law For Large Families," *The Jerusalem Post*, March 8, 1979.

Heller, Celia S. (1973). "The Emerging Consciousness of the Ethnic Problem Among the Jews of Israel," in Curtis, Michael, and Chertoff, Mordecai S. (editors), *Israel: Social Structure and Change*, Transaction Books, New Brunswick, New Jersey, 313-332.

Hoffert, Miriam. (1962). "Community Organization Practice," in *Saad*, 6:5, 188-192.

Jaffe, Eliezer D. (1978). "Project Renewal: A Caution," *Moment*, 3:9, 63-64.

_____ (1980a). "Not Just Charity," *The National Jewish Monthly*, 94:5, 32-33.

_____ (1980b). *Ethnic Preferences of Israelis*, unpublished manuscript, Jerusalem, 1-122.

Korazim, Josef (1978). "The Israeli Social Worker as a Social Warner," *Bitachon Sotziali*, 16:2, 124-131 (Hebrew).

Loewenberg, Frank M. (1978). "Social Work Education in Israel," in Spiro, S. (editor), *Issues and Explorations in Social Work Education*, Israel Association of Schools of Social Work, Tel Aviv, 4-8.

Neipris, Joseph. (1978). "Training and Education for Social Work Services in Israel," in Spiro, S. (editor), *Programs of Social Work Education in Israel*, Israel Association of Schools of Social Work, Tel Aviv, 1-8.

Prime Minister's Office (1974). "Voluntary Social Services," *Prime Minister's Report on Disadvantaged Children and Youth*, 2nd edition, Jerusalem, 1-28 (Hebrew).

Rein, Martin (1970). "Social Work in Search of a Radical Profession," *Social Work*, 15:2, 13-28.

Rosen, Harry M. (1979). *Volunteerism in Israel*, Jacob Blaustein Institute for the Advancement of Human Rights, The American Jewish Committee, New York.

Schmelz, Usiel O., editor (1976). *Society in Israel: Selected Statistics*, Central Bureau of Statistics, Jerusalem.

Smooha, Sammy (1978). *Israel: Pluralism and Conflict*, University of California Press, Berkeley.

Spergel, Irving (1975). "The Role of the Community Worker," in Kramer, Ralph M., and Specht, Harry (editors), *Readings in Community Organization Practice*, Prentice-Hall, Englewood Cliffs, New Jersey.

York, Alan S. (1978). "A Course for Volunteer Organizers," in Spiro, S. (editor), *Issues and Explorations in Social Work Education*, Israel Association of Schools of Social Work, Tel Aviv, 105-107.

ABOUT THE AUTHOR

Prof. Eliezer D. Jaffe has lived in Israel since 1960. He was trained in the United States, taking degrees in sociology, psychology, criminology and his doctorate in social work. Since emigrating to Israel, he has taught at the Hebrew University, chiefly at its Paul Baerwald School of Social Work. He has been a consultant to the Israel Ministry of Social Welfare and has served on several Ministerial Committees including the Prime Minister's Committee on Disadvantaged Youth and the Committee to Determine Israel's Poverty Line. Between 1970 and 1972, he headed the Jerusalem Municipal Department of Family and Community Services, introducing major reforms, many of which have since been adopted nationwide.

Dr. Jaffe's research has focused primarily on welfare services to children and their families. He is presently engaged in studying affirmative action models in Israeli social work education, philanthropy in Israel, and in an assessment of ethnic stereotypes and preferences among Israelis. He publishes frequently in professional journals and in the Israeli and American Jewish press and is the author of five books.

In 1976 Dr. Jaffe received the Bernard Revel Memorial Award, presented annually to the most outstanding scholar and community leader among the alumni of Yeshiva University. He is an independent, frank interpreter and analyst of social problems in Israel and an ardent advocate of involvement by Jews abroad in Israeli social affairs. He is a co-founder of Zahavi, the Israel Association of Large Families, a former member of the Central Committee of the Israel Association of Social Workers, an advisor and community organizer of social action groups, and Chairman of the Israel Committee of the New Israel Fund. Dr. Jaffe is Associate Professor of Social Work at the Hebrew University.

BOOKS BY ELIEZER JAFFE

Prof. of Social Welfare. The Hebrew University of Jerusalem

Child Welfare in Israel

A description, analysis, and critique of Israeli child welfare services. A resource and textbook by an expert who has been closely involved with developments in social work education, practice, and policy in Israel for over two decades.

Praeger Scientific Publishers, 521 Fifth Avenue, New York 1982, 319 pp., $21.95.

Giving Wisely: The Israel Guide to Non-Profit Volunteer Social Services in Israel

Detailed profiles of nearly 400 non-profit Israeli social service organizations desperately in need of funds. Few philanthropists have ever heard of many of them. Giving Wisely is the first effort to prevent a survival-of-the-fittest situation in which the more sophisticated organizations, often the wealthiest, win out.

The Jerusalem Post, 120 East 56 Street, N.Y.C. 10022, 656 pp., $18.00

Israelis in Institutions: Studies in Child Placement Practices and Policy

An inside view of the data and the debate over Israeli institutional care, the politics of child care and organizational survival, and major challenges confronting Israeli child welfare workers.

Gordon and Breach Science Publishers, Inc., One Park Avenue, New York 10016. 213 pp.

Pleaders and Protesters: The Future of Citizens' Organizations in Israel

Reports the changing roles, goals, and strategies of grassroots citizens' groups involved with social change in Israel; the implications of the Israeli Black Panther movement and the mass protests against the Government after the Yom Kippur War, and the social action groups.

The American Jewish Committee, 165 East 56 Street, New York, N.Y. 10022. 36 pp., $2.50

Letters to Yitz

This short volume traces the paths of two brothers who grew up in an immigrant Jewish family in the Midwest. The older brother, Yitz, raised a family and was a prominent, active member of his community, until his untimely and tragic death in 1978. This book is Eliezer Jaffe's dialog with his brother in their correspondence over nearly three decades. It will speak to those who have experienced close family ties, separation, and the loss of loved ones.

Herzl Press, 515 Park Avenue, New York, N.Y. 10022. 83 pp. $5.00.